About
Daniella Blechner

Daniella Blechner, author of *Mr Wrong*, is a South London based Writer/Director whose real writing journey began by creating comedy sketches for Youth Project *Phenomenon '98* featuring Gina Yashere and Richard Blackwood. She has always been a keen writer and penned her first books, *All the Happy Animals* and *Lucille and her Great Adventure*, at just 8 years old.

At 18 years old she began her career as a performance poet and enjoyed success in bars and clubs in and around London for many years. In 2002 she attended Ravensbourne College where she wrote, produced and directed her first short *Connexions* which was Nominated for Best Screenplay at the BFM Short Film Awards in 2006 and won "Best Open Deck Film" when screened at the Cutting East Festival.

Daniella won the 2007 Film Fund Award from Lewisham Film Initiative to complete her poetry based short drama, *Hair We Are*, for the Black History Month Short Film Challenge. Hair We Are won the 3rd Best Film at the Images of Black Women Film Festival and has been screened at Chicago International Children's film, Pan African Film Festival, LA and BAMKids Film Festival in New York. It was also screened on The Community Channel. Since writing and directing the film the poem has been included in Nicole Moore's Shangwe H*air Power, Skin Revolution* anthology.

She is also the author of poetry anthology *7 Shades of Love*, "an eclectic mix of poems written from women and men across the world exploring the Universal theme of Love."

Daniella enjoys examining and reflecting on social issues often laced with a wicked sense of humour. She especially enjoys working with young people and those "at risk" for exclusion from society.

www.daniellablechner.com
www.dingdongitsmrwrong.com
info@daniellablechner.com

Mr Wrong Workbook

*Break the pattern
of attracting Mr Wrong*

Daniella Blechner

Mr Wrong Workbook: Daniella Blechner.

Non Fiction Self Help

Copyright © 2015 by Daniella Blechner

Printed in the United Kingdom

First Printing 2014.Conscious Dreams Publishing. Daniella Blechner.

ISBN
www.daniellablechner.com
www.dingdongitsmrwrong.com

The Many Shades of Mr Wrong AKA 'The Mr Wrong Manual.'

First of all I think it's essential I share with you my Mr Wrong manual. The Mr Wrong Manual acts as a beacon of light that allows us to identify Mr Wrong and is a physical reminder to stop denying what we may know deep inside. Sometimes, even though we've been presented with inklings and hints (huge hints dropped down from the High Heavens!) we still try to turn that frog into a Prince,...and not just any old Prince but a Prince that would meet all our expectations. Why do we women do this? Is it because we love to fix and change, is it because the truth of the matter is too painful to absorb and makes us feel unworthy or is it that we have such a blinkered view of things we would say the sky is green rather than face up to the fact we have met and let in another Mr Wrong? Whatever the reason, The Mr Wrong Manual is great to use whilst dating and can help get you clear about what you don't want so that you can focus on what you do. If you find yourself attracting a particular type of Mr Wrong, this is a great time to start examining what it is that is drawing them to you or vice versa.

Nearly every woman, myself included, has experienced a Mr Wrong, to one extent or another and I'm sure that as you look through the Mr Wrong Manual you'll find yourself thinking, "I know him!" or "That was my ex!" This doesn't mean we have to go out and shove the manual in their face to prove how wrong they are; this is a practical and fun tool for you to use in recognising the type of men you attract in order to move you into a space of self-discovery and progression. This manual and workbook comes from a place of empowerment but we will also have a little fun along the way!

An interesting idea could be to look at how we may reflect some of the traits these characters display as often we attract people who highlight things within ourselves. For example, all of these men are unavailable: emotionally available. If you are continually attracting men who are emotionally unavailable, it's a great idea to look at where you might be emotionally unavailable or what "availability" means to you. If you continually meet Mr Serial Liar, it's useful to look at where you have been lied to in your past and what truth and honesty mean to you. How far on your list of values is it really?

Without further ado, I am about to reveal to you the 8 main characters that make up the Many Shades of Mr Wrong. Some you may recognise and some you may pray you never meet. Most importantly, by identifying them, we can recognise them more easily when they present themselves and make the conscious decision to set out for Mr Right for You instead.

Mr Drifter

Appearance:

Wears a glazed expression and a permanent yet annoyingly content smile.

Movement:

Strolls instead of walks, often nods head and closes his eyes with said content smile glued to his face. On exiting the relationship, his movement is like a piece of driftwood floating in a canal.

Typical Phrase:

"I'll do it in a minute."
"I dunno really."
"How did I get here?!"

Tone of Voice:

Often low and quiet, sometimes as if barely speaking at all.

The Drifters fickly float about with no real aim or purpose.

• They flit from one 'relationship' to another, never quite knowing what they are seeking.
• They may have lots of different hobbies but none they really stick at or see through.
• They are jacks-of-all-trades and masters of none. We are attracted to their easy-going nature and laid-back approach—until we realise that "laid back approach" we initially loved is actually aloof on a whole new level and is apathy incarnated. These types are prone to drifting into relationships and even marriages not quite knowing how or why they got there.
• Mr Drifter may have spent time "kipping on sofas" or travelling around "finding himself."
• Mr Drifters often search for a mother figure to help them realise their dreams and you may be funding this dream.
• Mr Drifter could spend years in a relationship with you before realising that his dream is not to be a lawyer but to travel to Goa alone.

The woman on the receiving end of this may feel deeply betrayed and used. Don't let him

Mr Dreamer

Appearance:

Has a refined glow about him, a dashing smile, and hypnotic eyes.

Movement:

His movements are delicate, smooth, and precise. His movement on exit differs from Mr Drifter as he moves at the speed of lightning.

Typical Phrase:

"It's you and me all the way, baby."
"It's destiny that you and I met."
"Am I The One?"

Tone of Voice:

Silky and enchantingly smooth.

Mr Dreamer has lots of dreams, hopes, and ambitions but nothing written down on paper.

• Mr Dreamer is often a charming man with a silver tongue and silky words that could convert the greatest cynic into a dedicated disciple.
• Mr Dreamer lures his woman with fanciful words, flattery, and flamboyant ideas for the future.

He will sweep you off your feet and into his cloud. However, sooner or later you're wading through a cloud of dust, wondering where he has gone. It is then that you realise that he has no real intention of settling down, landing that dream job, putting that sparkly ring on your finger, walking you down that aisle, being that fantastic father he never had, or growing old together with you. Did he ever exist, or was he a mere illusion? Leave well alone!

Mr Surfer

Appearance:

Wears a happy-go-lucky smile and placid expression.

Movement:

Moves quickly and quietly as he darts from one place to the other, swiftly serving and escaping "confrontation" and any perceived trouble.

Typical Phrase:

"We can talk about it later, hon."
"We don't need to talk about it right now."
"What do you mean I'm surfing all over your feelings?"

Tone of voice:

Quiet, smooth, and calm. Talks as if coaxing a Rottweiler into being amiable.

Mr Surfer is a happy-go-lucky chap who enjoys the company of women but not the reality that being in a relationship brings.

• Mr Surfer has good intentions but no interest in talking about "feelings" or discussing "issues."
• He glosses over issues and problems and pretends that they do not exist.
• As he surfs over the waves, he causes unknown havoc. He may wound his partner with his words or actions but refuses to talk about the repercussions or implications of them.
• His fear of confrontation or adult discussions causes breakdowns in communication, leaving his other half feeling unheard and unappreciated. She is made to feel like a 'nag' or that her feelings are unimportant while resentment grows deep inside her.

This lack of communication and this lack of willingness to take responsibility or to listen with compassion creates a woman who bears, deep inside, the angry Rottweiler Mr Surfer so desperately fears.

Mr Loose Eye

Appearance:

Large goggle eyes and gormless expression. Often has his mouth open and has a tendency to dribble.

Movement:

Shifty, revolving eyes and a revolving head that can turn a full owl-like 360!

Typical Phrase:

"I'm just looking at her T-shirt!"
"What were you saying?"
"Why are you always accusing me!"

Tone of Voice:

Soft and reassuring.

This guy has a revolving eye! Whilst looking you in the eye and telling you you're the best thing since sliced bread, his revolving eye scans the area for a sandwich! This one is easy to spot; it's the darting eyes, snatching furtive looks at any attractive female within his range or the greedy licking of lips, like a kid in a candy store about to dip his hand into the pic 'n' mix trough. Other giveaways are the blatant goggle eyed, dropped jaw, and gormless gawp over your shoulder as he puts his hand on your knee 'reassuringly.' Unless you like to 'share', he isn't for you. Leave well alone!

Mr Workaholic

Appearance:

Small, tired eyes, a tense expression. Rarely smiles. Often has a throbbing vein located at right temple.

Movement:

He dashes about like a bolt of lightning attending to his work needs, but slobs about at home.

Typical Phrase:

"I'm working late again, honey."
"In early tomorrow."
"I can't make it. I'm working."

Tone of Voice:

Busy, rushed, and tense.

Mr Workaholic, at the start, shows bundles of commitment, responsibility, and reliability; however, pretty soon you find he has no intention of marrying you because he is already married to his job.

• Usually this man runs about working all the hours God sends, working on one project after another, running around after everyone else to cover up his deep-rooted sense of insecurity and fear of commitment to another human being.
• He is the trusted and dependable employee or boss and commitment-phobic boyfriend, lover, or husband.
• Even when he is not working, he creates work so that he can avoid any real attachment he may feel towards you.

He will always put work first, leaving you at the bottom of the pile wondering why you need to compete with his job. Get rid. Job done!

Mr Serial Liar

Appearance:

Not everything that glitters is gold.

Movement:

Has a shifty, rat-like nervousness about him. His movements are quick and sharp as he ducks and dives as if dodging a bullet. Often coughs to cover up his lies and scratches his head and nose. Prone to twitching and head turning as he scans the area for trails of his lies.

Typical Phrase:

"Honest, babe."
"It's not you, it's me."
"You're the only one for me."

Tone of Voice:

Amateur—changes pitch and tone frequently. Professional—has a slow and steady, reassuring tone.

Mr Serial Liar has a disillusioned existence. In fact, he is so disillusioned that he actually believes his lies. Have you ever had a man, whilst gazing into your eyes, tell you—and actually convince you—that the sky was green? Well, this is he.

• This man has no qualms about looking you in the eyes and, despite being asked for honesty, repeats a lie over and over again until you are brainwashed into believing it.
• This man may have multiple girlfriends or may even be married, yet he is able to convince you otherwise, making you out to be 'psycho' or 'mad' for not believing his priceless porkies.

These men are duplicitous and deceitful. They want to have their cake and eat it and have you watch them too. These men are the most pitiful as they are afraid to live in reality and to face their own truths. Let sleeping dogs lie and take a hike!

Mr Ex Factor

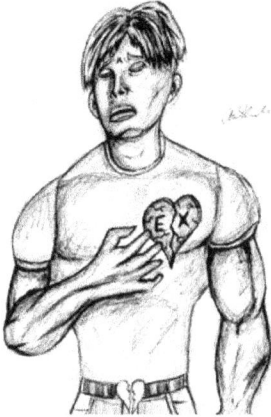

Appearance:

Wears a permanent pained expression as if he's had an unfortunate encounter with a liquor of laxatives.

Movement:

Walks slowly with shoulders stooped; he's a broken man trapped in a time warp.

Typical Phrase:

"I'm over her."
"She needs me."
"Me and my ex used to go here."

Tone of Voice:

Monotonous and whiny.

This man is not available. He says he wants to move on, yet "Ex" seems to be the only word coming out of his mouth.

• He constantly compares you to her, speaks to her, plays the concerned ex-boyfriend by helping out with odd jobs, and is there for her.
• If he's not speaking to her, he talks to you about the pain he went through and is still going through, saying she cheated on him and broke his heart.

You are forever feeling second best, and every time he's with you, you can read his mind as he checks his phone to see if she's called. You are so far down on his list of priorities he may even forget to call and to cancel dates. He may make false promises and apologise yet lets you down time and time again. This man is not—I repeat, is not—available. He will never give you the love, security, or attention you deserve because he is still hung up on his ex! Make a swift ex-it!

Mr Parasite

Appearance:

Looks shiny on the outside. Looks are irrelevant as they are deceiving, but if you look close enough, you can see the hooked claws, translucent skin, and sharp fangs beneath his smiling mouth.

Movement:

Walks as if he is drained of all energy before feeding yet buzzing with excitement after.

Typical Phrase:

"I'm not blaming you, but it's your fault."
"We need to talk. You've upset me again."
"I didn't ask for this drama. You made me do it."

Tone of Voice:

Will use any tone of voice necessary to get required 'emotion' across. Often has an accusatory/defensive tone.

Mr Parasite is the most dangerous of all. There are two types to watch out for. Emotionally draining parasites, sometimes known as 'drainers,' are usually jealous, possessive, or insecure types who need constant control and power.

• They'll gain your heart by exposing their emotional side to you in the hope you'll do the same. Before you know it, they've managed to expose your vulnerabilities, doubts, and insecurities so that they can refer to and feed off these later.

For example, if you tell them you fear abandonment, they'll threaten to dump you and leave you every time you do something they don't want you to do. Let's say you go to a party with the girls or go on girls' holiday. Their own deep-seated insecurity and fear of abandonment is transferred onto you.

Another example could be that, after having told them you have been betrayed before, they go out of their way to make you feel as if they could cheat on you if you displease them. They feed off your insecurities in order for them to grow taller, more powerful. This is, knowingly or not, emotional abuse. Emotionally needy parasites drain your time, energy, and love for fear that you will abandon them.

• They need constant validation and reassurance and, in doing so, form an unhealthy attachment to you, whereby you become his private supply of all that's positive in his life.
• These men often cause dramas, arguments, and traumas in a desperate attempt to keep the relationship alive by creating urgent and dramatic situations that constantly demand your attention.

A man must love himself before he can love another. A man must be secure in himself before he can provide security and equally share love with another. This is a sorry situation, and you will always be his source of energy until you create boundaries and a sense of personal space with this type of man. Better still. Power up and find Mr Right.

These Men Are Unavailable

These men all have one thing in common. They are UNAVAILABLE, whether it is emotionally, mentally, or physically. In light of this, one thing is for sure: if we learn from them and move on, we can grow from them both in strength and in wisdom. We may dwell on the pain and misery they have caused us, but perhaps there is one thing we can thank Mr Wrong for: if we can identify him quickly enough and finally stop blaming and battering ourselves for not getting Mr Wrong to love us, we can recognise exactly what it is we don't want and start focussing on exactly what it is we do!

We are the author of our own destiny, and we make the conscious decisions as to who and enters our lives. Our life is a blank canvass. We are given the tools to paint, create, decorate, erase, remould, and reshape it in any way we see fit. Everything within our unique canvass is there only because we have put or allowed it to be there. If a relationship is making you unhappy, change it. If a man is making you feel unloved or unworthy, remove him from your life. If you feel you've put up with too much for too long, don't beat about the bush, don't spend hours complaining to the girls about how awful your life is. Reshape it, steer it in a different direction, and set out on a path to "Mr Right."

"Everything in your life is a reflection of a choice you have made. If you want a different result, make a different choice."- unknown

1. Values

Everyone has values and these values vary from person to person. The word "value" derives from the Old French, feminine past participle of valoir 'be worth' and originates from Latin valere. Values are the core beliefs and principles that you live by or a personal "moral code". Just as the word value comes from the word "worth" our values should reflect what we deem to be worthy.

How many of us have focussed on or have been influenced by society's ideals of having a "tall, dark and handsome" time and time again and ended up with a good looking Mr Wrong? Are we focussing on just the exterior or do we have deeper values beyond that? How clear are you on your own values? It's easy to assume that Mr Good-Looking will treat you like a Princess and be the man of your dreams, however how important is getting to know a man and examine his values and beliefs about love and relationships?

When we know our values we are better equipped to attract men who reflect these values. I once went on a few dates with a guy who I got on with very well. On date 3 he told me that he would disown his own son if he found out he was gay. Seeing that he was deadly serious, I knew I could not continue dating this man. To me, support, love and acceptance of our loved ones for who they are without judgement, is very high up on my list of values. It is essential for me to be with someone who loves their children unconditionally. This told me that anything that goes against his own limited beliefs of what he thought was 'right' warranted punishment. Even though I thought he was a great person (bar this) and was physically attracted to him, I could never be with someone who was okay with abandoning their own child. Love should not be conditional and certainly should not be withheld from your own children. This completely went against my own value system and there was never a date 4!

Having very similar values is fundamental to compatibility. It's one of the key elements that hold us together. We may not have identical values to our partner's however respecting each other's values is essential. Remember, just as the word value means worth, it's important to find someone who sees your values and beliefs as worthy of respect just as you are worthy, too.

What Are Your Values?

E.g. It is important for me to be with someone who respects women (hopefully that's all of us. It's important for me to be with someone who wants to date before being physical.

1. _____
_____

2. _____
_____

3. _____
_____

4. _____
_____

5. _____
_____

6. _____
_____

7._____
_____

8. _____
_____

9. _____
_____

10. _____
_____

Needs, Wants and Desires

Needs, wants and desires are very essential in relationships. Everybody has needs, wants and desires that they would like to be fulfilled. The question is how often do we remember them? Have they ever been written down? In some cases they haven't even been recognised or identified until we are treated badly.

What are the Differences between Needs, Wants and Desires?

Needs are essential prerequisites we require to survive in a situation. They are the basics as it were, qualities or things we cannot do without. For example we all have a basic need to be loved healthily and a basic need for respect.

Wants are things we would like but will still survive without. For example I want a car but as I live in London and am close to an abundance of transport links I do not NEED one desperately. However wants in relationships are again essential as we are choosing and setting intentions regarding the kind of relationship and man we want.

Desires are add-ons, things we really, really want but can live without. They are luxuries that we crave and deep down dream of and yearn for. For example I desire to go to Cuba this summer, visit Brazil and camp out in the Amazon, however practicalities and real life means that I may not necessarily get to do these things. Desires are something to aim for and never give up on. Look at the example exercise below and try it for yourself. Don't worry if you become stuck or are not sure what you need, want and desire. This exercise will get you thinking and setting your expectations and intentions. Go for it! You deserve to be fulfilled!

Exercise

Needs, Wants and Desires

What Do I Need?

I need a man who respects me.
I need a man who is reliable.
I need a man who is kind and generous, loving and affectionate.

I need a relationship that is equal.
I need a relationship that is based on trust.
I need a relationship that is happy and healthy.

What Do I Want?

I want a man who will take me out on dates regularly.
I want a man listens to me compassionately.
I want a man who supports and encourages me.

I want a relationship that has plenty of laughter.
I want a relationship that is full of passion.
I want a relationship where each other listens

What Do I Desire?

I desire a man who pampers me with massages and foot rubs once in a while.
I desire a man who takes me out on romantic dates.
I desire a man who enjoys travelling to exotic locations with me.

I desire a relationship that is full of romance, passion and love.
I desire a peaceful yet exciting romantic relationship that results in a long term marriage.
I desire a relationship where we travel extensively and enjoy exploring all corners of the Earth.

Exercise
Needs, Wants and Desires

What Do I Need?

I need a man who _____.
I need a man who _____.
I need a man who _____.

I need a relationship _____.
I need a relationship _____.
I need a relationship _____.

What Do I Want?

I want a man who _____.
I want a man who _____.
I want a man who _____.

I want a relationship _____.
I want a relationship _____.
I want a relationship _____.

What Do I Desire?

I desire a man who _____.
I desire a man who _____.
I desire a man who _____.

I desire a relationship _____.
I desire a relationship _____.
I desire a relationship _____.

3. First Loves

The Interactive First Love Quiz

Try the Interactive First Love Quiz. Sometimes it is good to reflect on our past relationships in order to recognise any reoccurring patterns or changes we have made to our lives. Sometimes we need to get perspective to see how far we've come, to reflect upon our own journeys. The quiz below will help you to identify any reoccurring themes/ patterns/attractions that may be helping you forward or perhaps holding you back. Try to answer the questions as honestly as you can and see what conclusions you draw. Enjoy!

First Love to Last Love Quiz

How old were you when you first met your first love?	How old are you now?
Where did you meet your first love?	Where did you meet your first/current love?
What did you look for in a man?	What do you look for in a man now?
What first attracted you to your first love?	What first attracted you to your last/current love?
What was your happiest memory together?	What was/are your happiest memory with your last/current partner?
What were your dreams/goals and ambitions when you were with your first love? Career? Love life?	What are your dreams/goals and ambitions now?

What were the positive qualities of your first love?	What are the positive qualities in your last/ current partner?
What were the negative/unattractive qualities in your first love?	What were/are the negative/unattractive qualities in your last/current love?
What would your first love say your positive qualities were?	What would your last/current love say your positive qualities were?
What would your first love say your negative/ unattractive qualities were?	What would your last/current love say your negative/unattractive qualities were?
If you argued, what did you argue about?	If you argue/d, what did you argue about?
On a scale of 1-10, how confident were you?	On a scale of 1-10, how confident were/are you?
How did you feel about yourself then?	How did you feel about yourself in your last relationship/now?
What were the negative aspects of your relationship?	What were/are the negative aspects of your relationship?

What were the positive aspects of your relationship?	What are the positive aspects of your relationship?
If you could change anything in your relationship, what would you change?	If you could change anything in your relationship, what would you change?

Reflective Questions

What has changed?

_____

_____

_____

What's stayed the same?

_____

_____

_____

What would you like to change?

_____

_____

_____

How are you going to change it?

_____

_____

_____

4. The Dating Game

There's no "two ways" about it; dating is back in fashion. With the rise of the internet, internet dating is a fast growing phenomenon worldwide. According to The Huffington Post, online dating is a £2bn industry. With over half of the UK's singletons internet dating, Huffington Post[1] states, "Online dating is now so important to the UK economy that the Office of National Statistics recently added online dating to its basket of goods and services to calculate UK inflation rates." Globally one in five relationships start via online dating and there are constantly stories in the media detailing happy marriages sparked by online dating subscriptions. With over 7'500 sites available globally, online dating can be a great way to connect people to each other from all over the world, match people with similar likes, dislikes, interests and relationship needs and wants.

Whilst there has been much success online, there are also plenty of fish to wade though. The anonymity that comes with online profiles sadly means that it gives room for people to masquerade behind false images and personas. How many of you have met a well-oiled "personal training" Adonis' who turned out to be a beer swigging, beer bellied IT consultant? I have nothing against beer swigging, beer bellied IT consultants, however this is not who they said they were. I always think it's best to be completely honest about who you are and what you want right from the start. How many women have gone out with men who blatantly state that they are "not looking for anything serious" then get upset when they don't want a full-blown relationship? The proof is in the pudding- black and white. If a man says he doesn't want a relationship it means he doesn't want a relationship. Equally if ultimately you do want a serious relationship, don't say you're "just looking for fun." Honesty and transparency make the dating game much easier!

Another 'don't' when building an online profile is don't tell readers what you don't want, tell them what you do. The amount of profiles (men in this case) that read, "'Don't' message me without a picture", "'Don't' want a woman who nags", "'Don't' want any dramatists", "'Don't' want negative women not over their ex," is phenomenal. I'm a firm believer that what we give life to we receive. Focus on what you do want, not what you don't - you'll only get more of the same. Furthermore, by focussing on the thing that you desire, you will create a far clearer picture of exactly what it is you are looking for, and you'll come across as a far more positive person!

Some people say writing their profile is the hardest part of online dating. A profile should take time and thought. There is nothing worse than reading a profile that says "wanna know just ask." Taking time and effort shows that you are serious about dating and want to meet someone compatible with who you are. Profiles that say "wanna know just ask," not only demonstrates laziness and makes the user look dull, but also makes the user seem as if they are expecting. Use the space below to create your own profile before committing to pressing "publish" online.

My Online Profile

Name: _____

Age: _____

Sex: (don't say "yes please!"): _____

Looking for(e.g. casual/dating/nothing):

_____

About Me:

_____

_____

_____

_____

_____

_____

Ideal partner/date:

_____

_____

_____

_____

_____

_____

Why Date?

Dating is essential when getting to know someone. Always take a dip with someone before diving in. Dating gives you the opportunity to really get to know the man you may end up in a relationship with. Through conversation and experiencing shared interests you can get to observe and learn different aspects of your date's personality, etiquette, and social skills in different settings. It also allows you to get insight into your date's values.

Dating should be fun and light and easy. It gives both parties an opportunity to get to know each other. Have a list of questions you want to ask or things you want to find out about your date and slip them in subtly but remember, whilst being cautious and taking your time is important when finding the right partner, it is equally important to ensure the person does not feel like they are in an interview or taking part in an assessment of some sort. Dating should take place in a relaxed environment where both parties can be themselves and feel at ease.

Before dating, it is a good idea to think about what sort of date you want. What would you like to do? Are you looking for a companion or for something more serious? What qualities do you look for in a man?

The Dating Quiz

What is your ideal date? E.g. Adventurous? Outdoors? Restaurant? Cinema? Give detail.

_____

_____

_____

What are the qualities you look for in a man?

_____

_____

_____

What values are important for you?

_____

_____

_____

What are the "red flags" for you?

_____

_____

_____

Have you ever spotted any of these red flags on the first few dates and carried on?

_____

_____

_____

How did the experience progress?

_____

_____

_____

Would you react differently now? How?

_____

_____

_____

What is the best date you've ever had and why?

_____

_____

_____

What do YOU bring to a date?

_____

_____

_____

Question Time!

What would you like to find out about your date before going on date number two? Write a list of 10 questions you would like to ask your date. Think about your values and what is important to you. NB. This does not mean you have to reel them off one after the other, interview style. Be discreet. Remember, these questions can always be answered during natural dialogue with your date. My top two questions would be as follows:

    1) Is family important to you?
    2) How do you usually spend your free time?

1) _____

2) _____

3) _____

4) _____

5) _____

6) _____

7) _____

8) _____

9) _____

10) _____

Now look back at these questions and write down the answers. Is this man compatible with you? Do his actions support his answers as time progresses?
Good Luck!

Date Diary

We all have busy lifestyles and this sometimes makes it difficult to reflect on our lives as a whole. Searching specific areas of our lives is even tougher. Keeping a Date Diary is a good idea as it gives you the opportunity to look back at your dates and evaluate how they've developed over time. It also helps you establish whether his "initial" or "first impression" behaviour is consistent over time. Often when we first meet someone we put on a face or a front to impress the other. This face usually drops after the first couple of dates when we feel more comfortable with one another.

Here's a classic example. I once went on a date with a man years ago who opened the doors and pulled out the chairs for me for the first few dates however after the fifth date, he left me to pull out my chair myself and practically let the door swing back in my face! If chivalry is important to this man, it would be naturally ingrained.

Consistency is the most important thing you should be looking for. No one can keep up their "game face" for very long unless that "game" is really who they are.

The next pages are for you to write your dating diary. Be sure to include what you spoke about, what you liked about your date and what you learned about his values and behaviour.

Date 1

_____

_____

_____

_____

_____

_____

_____

_____

_____

_____

_____

_____

_____

_____

_____

_____

_____

_____

Three words to describe the date.

_____

_____

_____

What was the highlight?

_____

_____

_____

What attracted you to him on this date?

_____

_____

_____

Record his gentlemanly act here.

_____

_____

_____

What would you change about the date?

_____

_____

_____

Anything you didn't like?

_____

_____

_____

Would you see him again?

_____

_____

_____

Other Notes:

Date 2

_____

_____

_____

_____

_____

_____

_____

_____

_____

_____

_____

_____

_____

_____

_____

_____

_____

_____

_____

Three words to describe the date.

_____

_____

_____

What was the highlight?

_____

_____

_____

What attracted you to him on this date?

_____

_____

_____

Record his gentlemanly act here.

_____

_____

_____

What would you change about the date?

_____

_____

_____

Anything you didn't like?

_____

_____

_____

Would you see him again?

_____

_____

_____

Other Notes:

Date 3

_____

_____

_____

_____

_____

_____

_____

_____

_____

_____

_____

_____

_____

_____

_____

_____

_____

_____

_____

_____

Three words to describe the date.

_____

_____

_____

What was the highlight?

_____

_____

_____

What attracted you to him on this date?

_____

_____

_____

Record his gentlemanly act here.

_____

_____

_____

What would you change about the date?

_____

_____

_____

Anything you didn't like?

_____

_____

_____

Would you see him again?

_____

_____

_____

Other Notes:

"Just Not that into You" Texts Exercise

Sometimes our dates just don't work out. Dates should be fun and light. It's safe space to meet someone new and get a feel for them. Sometimes you click, sometimes you don't. They could be the hottest thing since (insert favourite male celebrity here) but if they don't share the same fundamental values as you or want the same things then, you are just not compatible if you ultimately want a successful long term relationship. It may be a case that you just simply weren't attracted to him, which is fine, too, but one thing we shouldn't do is keep these men hanging or believing they have a chance when they don't. Just as we know how awful it can be to date somebody and suddenly never hear from them again, we, too, have a responsibility to provide our date with honesty and respect. I think short and sweet responses are best: complimentary (unless he was a total tool!) but candid.

My own standard default "Just Not into You" text is:

> "It was great to meet you. I think you are (fill in appropriate compliment if you have one!), and I really enjoyed (fill in accurate activity). However, unfortunately I don't think we clicked romantically. I wish you well finding your Ms Right."

I like this as it is non-emotional and not personal. You are simply thanking him for his time and appreciating his company but being honest about your intentions at the same time. You can only really receive a positive response to this unless your date decides to hit you with a barrage of texts telling you how wrong you are about your decision and that you DID click romantically, in which case block his number ASAP!

My 'Not Into You' Text

_____

_____

_____

_____

_____

Now type in your phone and press SEND![2]

---

2   That is of course if your date did not work out!!

5. When Men Lie

When we are lied to, it can be very damaging. If you have been continually lied to in the past by someone you once loved and trusted, then this can have some very negative effects. It can cause you to:

- Lose faith or trust in others
- Constantly question the veracity of what others may say or tell you
- Be suspicious of others' intentions.

Sometimes we try to turn lies into truths to suit our own needs or to fit in with what we want to believe. Sometimes we turn a blind eye to unsavoury behaviour or allow people to continually lie to us because the truth may appear to be too much to bear. For many, it is much easier to believe what someone else is telling us instead of facing the reality that they are being lied to or being made a fool of.

There is a Power that lies deep within us all and that is the Power to Discern; that small still voice inside us that can read signals and feel the vibrations of others. This is called our Intuition. Everyone is born with Intuition; however some are more open to listening to it than others.

How in tune are you with your Intuition?

- Our intuition or gut feeling is what guides us;
- It is what tells us whether situations, people or circumstances are good for us or not.

Often we choose to ignore our Intuition and instead create our own realities. This is certainly evident in my story Mr Duplicitous in Mr Wrong. I had various dreams and signals presented before me together with a gut feeling that clearly told me something was wrong, however I chose to bury my Intuition because listening to it would mean that I had to face up to the fact that I had been fooled the entire duration of our relationship. By creating my own reality, it was easier to feel in control rather than admitting that I had been deceived.

Listening to our Intuition is crucial. It is that little candle that burns inside of us; quiet and still and always has our best interests at heart. Take some time out sitting still and journeying within. How in tune are you with yourself and your Intuition? Your Intuition **NEVER** lies. Practise tuning in everyday, listen to your inner feelings, they will tell you everything you need to know about a person. This is not about being super judgemental but about assessing whether people or situations are good for you or not. Someone who constantly lies isn't good for you. Can you spot a Serial Liar?

QUIZ

Can You Spot a Serial Liar?

When a person is lying the evidence can usually be found in:

   a) Type of words that are used
   b) Non-verbal expression
   c) Pitch and tone of voice

The addition of an epilogue when recounting events is a sign of:

   a) A true story
   b) A false story
   c) Both

A person who is lying often recounts a story:

   a) Starting from the end and ending with beginning
   b) No sequential order
   c) Using strict chronological order

A false smile uses:

   a) All the muscles in the face
   b) Only the muscle around the eyes
   c) Only the muscles around the mouth

When recounting information liar will:

   a) Use limited hand gestures
   b) Over exaggerate hand gestures
   c) Sit on their hands

When lying a liar will often touch:

a) Chest, arms, hands
b) Face, mouth, throat
c) Legs, feet and ankles

A common gesture for a liar is:

a) Interlocking hands behind their head
b) Scratching their nose or ea
c) Nodding incessantly

When liar's story will:

a) Contain lots of emotion
b) Lack emotion
c) Contain lots of detail

Liars commonly leave out words like:

a) Pronouns- I, me, my
b) Adjectives- describing words like beautiful, amazing, exhilarating
c) Adverbs- slowly, happily, excitedly

A real smile uses:

a) Lower half of face
b) The muscles around the mouth area
c) All the muscles in the face

Answers on page 62.

6. Emotionally Unavailable Men

The Mr Wrongs featuring in the Mr Wrong book have all got one thing in common. These men are Emotionally Unavailable. The term "emotionally unavailable" usually refers to those who create barriers between themselves and others in an effort to avoid emotional intimacy.

These kinds of relationships can be very taxing and painful for the person involved with the E.U.M (Emotionally Unavailable Man.) E.U.Ms often leave their partner feeling very confused, distressed, unloved and neglected and they end up continually wondering whether they are in a relationship at all. The more you try to seek love from the E.U.M the further and further apart you become as he will begin to create distance within the relationship. Relationships with E.U.Ms is like two magnets continually repelling and attracting but never actually coming together for enough length of time to create a bond that is meaningful. Women involved with E.U.Ms often blame themselves for not being enough or worthy of being loved.

What causes E.U.M?

Let's face it; men are not typically wired to be overly emotional. They are wired to be practical and logical, think rationally and provide solutions. Women are more emotional in their responses and intuitive in their reactions. Yes, there are exceptions but I'm talking generally here. I don't want a man to cry with me whilst watching an emotional film, I want a man to pass me the tissues. In saying this everyone needs to feel love and affection from their partner; a sense of connection and intimacy. These men are unable to provide us with these things for many reasons such as:

- Unresolved childhood issues relating to attachment.
- The belief that if they demonstrate loving emotions they are somehow weak.
- Fear of commitment.
- Feelings of unworthiness or inadequacy.
- Unresolved relationship issues.

They are already attached/ or married. There is nothing to say that these men are bad or villains in anyway but everything about this list shouts "BEWARE!" You will never be able to "fix" a person or change them into the person you want them to be. Why live with a Commitmentphobe when you need and want stability and commitment? Relationships with E.UM will only bring heartbreak and pain until he tackles the issues.

Have you ever been with someone who is Emotionally Unavailable?

How did it make you feel?

_____

_____

_____

_____

_____

What signs were there?

_____

_____

_____

_____

_____

How did the relationship progress?

_____

_____

_____

_____

_____

How did it end?

_____

_____

_____

_____

How did you feel when it came to an end?

_____

_____

_____

_____

Top Ten Signs you are Dating an E.U.M

Physically Unavailable

Emotionally Unavailable Men are not just emotionally unavailable they are physically unavailable too. Pinning this man down is like a challenging quest to contact aliens in outer space. He may text and call whenever it suits him but is never around when you need him. This man will never help you with things that are important to you such as moving, birthdays, weddings and funerals. He will rarely attend social events with you as this will only confirm that you are indeed a committed couple. Perish the thought!

James Bond Air of Mystery

This man desperately wants to be some sort of hero in your life that you can't live without yet never really reveals enough about himself for you to truly know who he is. He will never share intimate details about himself such as past history, relationships, childhood or important events in his life. He prefers to create an air of mystery to keep you guessing and to keep you hooked. This mystery man is one closed book that you do not need to prise open. Leave on the shelf and write your own story!

Secrets and Lies

As demonstrated in Louise's story this man may lie about his life, his material possessions, financial situation, age and even his name! His life is a total fabrication constructed upon secrets and lies. This man may be so accustomed to his Pinocchio porkies that he forgets what he's told you. He may get ratty when you begin to question him and make you feel that you are paranoid. Don't let him spin his web of deceit around you and don't question yourself. If something is off, it's off! Trust your intuition. If you smell a rat then it's probably because you're dating one. Men like this lie to deny themselves of the fact that they are a real human being in a real relationship or may even be attached or already married.

Flattery and Cheeky Charm

These men will tell you the sun shines out of your backside. He will compliment your smile, your eyes and everything about you. These men have silver tongues and are well versed with those silky smooth words. It is easy to be taken in by these words however remember they are just that: words. When you start to question his actions is when the real man will surface. The fact that "You have the cutest bum he ever saw," or "eyes as deep as the ocean" will mean nothing once he pulls the curtain and exits offstage.

Intimacy Avoidance

Similar to secrets and lies these men avoid intimate questions that could lead to a sense of closeness with another. In order to maintain the façade, they must not let anyone in. They build walls and defences like a moat around their castle so that they do not ever appear vulnerable or needy towards another. Letting someone in is dangerous. Their deeply ingrained fear of being attacked or open to humiliation, loss or even the deepening of a closer emotional bond keeps them closed off to love. While the castle cries out for love the person in it screams, "Why commit to someone who could eventually abandon me when I could exist happily alone, right?" Why drown in a murky moat when you could find someone who is open to love, affection and commitment?

Lack of Commitment

E.U.Ms will never mention the dreaded C-word. The C-word is the fear of all fears, danger of all dangers. The C-word will bring pain and bring grief and bring an end to all happiness. Committing to another is like signing your life away. Who wants to be ball and chained when you can run free? Commitmentphobes fear commitments of all sorts: commitment to a plan, commitment to decisions, commitment to keeping promises and commitment to a person. Committing to something or someone means that a decision has to be made, reached and adhered too. Sticking at something means that there is no way out; no room for manoeuvre. He may now be forever at the mercy of the commitment he has made. This is the mother of all fears. How does he know he wants strawberry jam when he hasn't tasted the raspberry yet? These men are Commitmentphobes due to their negative beliefs about love, relationships and commitment. The Commitmentphobe may display signs of wanting a relationship but once the honeymoon phase is over and the rose tinted glasses have been taken off, the running shoes come on. The grass is always greener with a Commitmentphobe yet they fail to realise that the reason the grass fades is because they are walking all over it!

Conversely, Commitmentphobes can be quite loving and affectionate but this is because they know the relationship isn't going to last. This is in line with their 'live fast die young' attitude. Commitmentphobes don't tend to have stable jobs or stable lives because they fear making any kind of stable decision.

Severe Commitmentphobes may actually love the woman they are with and fight hard to win her over. However when he eventually gets the woman of his dreams, he can never commit to staying. At the same time, he is unable to walk away completely. The woman is left feeling totally and utterly confused and may feel she is going insane. I can assure you, you are not. Whilst you may love Mr Commitmentphobe and he you, will he ever be able to provide you with the security and stability your relationship needs?

Unreliability

In line with the E.U.Ms' actions, they are completely unreliable. You can never count on these men for anything. They may promise to call or pick you up and forget or find something more important to do. They do things according to their schedule, not yours or 'ours'. They are often late to meet you or cancel plans and dates you have arranged. E.U.Ms are often unreliable because of their fear of commitment, fear of becoming too close or perhaps he has plans with his wife!

Wants to Get Physical Far Too Quickly

Sex is often the basis of the relationship. They may convince you that you belong together and that sex will cement the relationship or that it is more important than other aspects. Don't get me wrong the sex may be undeniably good but will more likely last as long as the relationship! Sex is a physical act rather than an emotionally intimate one in these cases. Think Daniel Cleaver in Bridget Jones and his desperate escape in the morning following Bridget's confession of love.

Random Acts of Disappearance

They will give you just enough to keep you hanging, putting in appearances here and there but not enough to create a sense of an actual relationship between you. If you ask him to meet your friends and family he may disappear for weeks on end in a puff of smoke. He may be on the phone to you every day one week then disappear for a weeks at a time. Random Acts of Disappearance or R.A.Ds are common themes in E.U.M[1] relationships. Too much closeness all at once is just too much and so R.A.Ds are essential for breathing space. Sometimes Batman is so exhausted from wearing his costume that he needs a good old cup of cocoa and feet up in his comfortable home that you probably haven't been to!

Boomerang Boy Behaviour

Boomerang Boys are boys who drift in and out of your life with no announcement or even goodbye. They charm you with hearts and flowers then disappear out of your life with no

---

[1]   It is important to note that being Emotionally Unavailable is not gender specific. Emotionally Unavailable simply means not being emotionally or physically present to provide the love, trust, security and stability a relationship needs.

warning, however just as soon as you start to get on with your life, just like magic, he's back!

Boomerang Boy will offer heartfelt apologies and promise you that he's changed. He may even tell you he has no hidden agenda and becomes your best friend and confidante. You tell him all the ins and outs of your life with your boyfriend and he listens compassionately telling you how much you deserve better (forgetting of course that he ran off with your best friend and had a whirlwind secret affair). Of course Boomerang Boy is there to offer a shoulder to cry on when it all falls to pieces and "hey presto" he's wormed his way back into your life! Don't get me wrong there are Boomerang Boys who can be Soulmates. The ones where you just can't live without and no matter what happens, the Universe will always pull you back together. I am not talking about these types of Boomerang Boys. I am talking about the ones who like to come and go. The ones who like to enter your life in a helicopter and leave through the back door. These are usually Emotionally Unavailable Men who cannot and will not go the distance with you yet don't want to let you go completely. The attachment they feels is comfortable and suits their needs as they do not ever have to fully commit.

Write down your Top Five Signs

1) _____

_____

2) _____

_____

3) _____

_____

4) _____

_____

5) _____

_____

Why do we Select these Men?

We may select these men because we are attracted to the sense of mystery surrounding them or the charm they exude. These men can conceal their true identity. They believe they can be anything they want to be to you. They often exude such charm we want to hop on the ride and see where it takes us. However, five months or even five years down the line the reality is we have been left high and dry in a game of merry-go-round with little but a sense of low self-esteem and a load of baggage he left us.

We may choose these men because perhaps we are attracted to his bad-boy image believing we can pin him down and be the one to 'change' him. He becomes the latest project. How many of us want to be the girl to change James Bond or tame Batman? We sometimes become so embroiled in the mystery and sense of 'wildness' he projects we become obsessed with ripping off his costume and revealing the true Self. The question we need to ask ourselves is: would we be so enamoured with the "boy-next-door?" I think if we discovered Batman was just plain Billy from the block we would be hugely disappointed.

Some women are attracted to E.U.M because they pity them or want to save them in some way. Again why attempt to fix that which is broken at the risk of breaking yourself? Trying to fix those we are in a relationship with always comes with conditions. The real reason we want to fix a man is so that they can become the person we want them to be for us. When we try to fix with these conditions we will always be the ones who will be broken. We form a co-dependant relationship where we live a life without boundaries and cater so heavily to the E.U.Ms needs we totally abandon our own!

Finally, we may attract these men because perhaps we ourselves are Emotionally Unavailable. We attract into our experience what we reflect. Our stories of emotional baggage and unresolved attachment issues may resonate so deeply with each other that you become two magnets bashing ferociously together and abruptly swinging apart in a two way game of hide and seek. There may be an attachment of some sort, however neither party is emotionally nor physically available to provide the other with the stability and commitment that a meaningful relationship needs.

Exercise

A good exercise to try is to divide a blank A4 piece of paper in two. On one side write a list of your needs and on the other what he is actually providing in relation to that need. That way you can have a crystal clear reality check that measures and identifies your needs in relation to what you are actually getting. Sometimes it is easy to believe that because a need may have been met once or twice then everything is alright, so it is also important to assess how regularly that need is being met. For example, it may be important to spend time together with your partner but if that need lacks consistency then is that really enough for you? It is important to be honest about our needs and not to forget their value.

What I Need	What I'm Getting

Write a Letter to your E.U.M Letting Him go.

Dear_____

_____

_____

_____

_____

_____

_____

_____

_____

_____

_____

_____

_____

_____

_____

_____

_____

7. Forgiveness

The key to living freer, happier and lighter lives is forgiveness. Forgiveness is such an easy word to say but sometimes so hard to do. Read the excerpt below from Mr Wrong.

Love Bless and Release

"Sometimes we experience so much pain we find it difficult to let go. We find it difficult to forgive and move on leaving us stuck in a negative cycle. However it is we who are weighed down and filled with bitterness, resentment, anger, disappointment and regret whilst whoever hurt us is walking around as light as a feather or perhaps continuing to treat others in the same hurtful way. Why are we carrying around their baggage? For hurt and pain are only inflicted as a result of others' insecurities. Ladies why are we carrying these bags??! What's in the past is in the past and must stay there! This is easier said than done. Sometimes we carry this burden - and believe you me I've carried a heavy load for a long, long time (probably the cause of my back pain) - because we are afraid to let go. We may feel that if we let go we are allowing the other person to "get away with it" or that we have become a "walkover" somehow by forgetting about it. But in essence what we are doing is quite the opposite; we are finally moving on without the load, without the negative thoughts and feelings eroding our backs, our emotions and our Souls. We also may feel that we cannot let go as we become quite nostalgic about the past. The abuse or pain we endured becomes less "valid" if we let it go. It defines us in some way and we don't want to forget it. But in actual fact what it's doing is making us move slower, making us weaker, bitter and lonely. Let that traumatic and painful part of your journey not define you but serve as a tool to help you grow stronger and wiser, happier and lighter. Again easier said than done.

Remember forgiving does not mean forgetting. It does not mean letting them back into your lives with the same circumstances or at all for that matter. It means seeing that person as a human being who's made some terrible mistakes but helped you grow in some way whether it was emotionally, physically, mentally or spiritually. For in every challenge or difficulty there is strength and wisdom to be gained. It means releasing that person and their negative energy, and the negative situation you endured from your own and freeing yourself. It means forgiving yourself for not feeling strong enough, being wise enough to react or acting differently at the time. Once forgiveness is achieved we can finally take the next step to finding true happiness and Mr Right. Without forgiveness we will keep attracting the same circumstances, same lessons and same type of person into our lives until forgiveness is learnt."

Now are you ready to forgive?

Think of someone who has hurt you. When you think of them, how do you feel in your body? Do your muscles start to tense up, does your throat become blocked with repressed emotion or does your brain start ticking about all the injustices you endured? Now is the time to let it go.

What do you need to forgive them for?

E.g. 1) I forgive you for not being there when I needed you.

Your Forgiveness List

1) _____

2) _____

3) _____

4) _____

5) _____

6) _____

7) _____

Now think about how holding this has made you feel over the weeks, months or years. Every negative emotion is felt in the body. It pollutes the mind and emotions and can start to wreak havoc on the body. It also blocks and creates stagnation in the natural flow of your energy system. If we could see the damage unforgiveness causes we would be apologising and forgiving ourselves. When we start to forgive ourselves we start to take ownership for what happened to us and recognise how we can act as our own angels. We can guide our own stories onto positive paths without repeating our victim story. What we are angry about is not so much the actual action itself but how it made us feel.

I Forgive Myself For...

1) Allowing what happened to me dictate how I feel about myself and the stories I have created as a result. I needed you but I also needed to be there for myself.

2) _____

3) _____

4) _____

5) _____

6) _____

7) _____

One of my favourite quotes is from visionary guide and spiritual teacher Sonia Choquette.

"Forgive and forget all that has hurt you in the past and made you doubt your own "lovability". Realise that hurt and disappointment are inevitable parts of our human learning experience. No matter how painful, the real injury was not that someone didn't cherish you, but that you erroneously believed you didn't deserve to be loved."

- Soul Lessons and Soul Purpose Oracle Cards- Sonia Choquette

Other Forgiveness Exercises

1) Write a letter to the person who has hurt you letting you know how you feel. When you have finished. Imagine them receiving it and fully listening and understanding what you have written with compassion and asking for your forgiveness. Let it go. Burn or throw away the letter. You are done. Keeping the letter keeps the negative emotions and energy alive.

2) Imagine a scenario where you are face to face with this person. Create a warm and peaceful atmosphere. Before you speak stare into their eyes and seek understanding and compassion. See their life, their hardships their struggles, see their beauty as well as their ugly behaviour, and see their pain as well as their triumphs. They are human just like you. Now tell them softly why you are hurting and how their actions or behaviour made you feel. See them listening to every word you say, taking it in. You have been heard and understood. You see in their eyes that somewhere along the lines, they too have been hurt and were only acting on and operating from their own level of understanding and painful experiences. Softly, they ask for your forgiveness and this is all you require. You accept. It is done. Peacefully, you both rise up, smile and walk your separate ways.

3) **Ho'oponopono** (ho-o-pono-pono) is an ancient Hawaiian practice of reconciliation and forgiveness. It is defined in the Hawaiian dictionary as "mental cleansing." Ponopono is defined as "to put to rights; to put in order or shape, correct, revise, adjust, amend, regulate, arrange, rectify, tidy up, make orderly or neat"[1]

How to do it: **Ho'oponopono** is a very simple ancient mantra which can be done by repeating this simple cycle of statements:

> I Love You,
> I'm Sorry,
> Please Forgive Me,
> Thank You

The purpose behind this is to reflect the belief that our purpose here is to let go and allow Love to solve our problems. Sound Good? Give it a whirl!

---

[1]　　Cited from Wikipedia

8. Have Fun!!

What I've come to realise in my old age is that Life really is short. It can be taken away from us at a moment's notice and suddenly, not getting that job, being cheated on or that argument with the ex becomes null and void. We think that we will live forever and that we are invincible; that our lives and what happens in them is so important. When this is all taken away or threatened, we realise that very few things are important. When I die I want God to ask me, "Did you Live enough?" "Did you Love enough? Did you **allow** enough LOVE in? Did you learn to forgive? Did you Laugh enough? Did you have Fun?" For these are the basis of every bit of positivity we can create within our lives. Passing a bit of Love onto another, even a stranger can be the making of their day. It can determine whether they take their lives that evening or tell someone they love them; it can determine whether they scream at their employees or bring cookies in to raise morale. We underestimate the power of a smile.

At one point or other we have all been saints or sinners. That's' the beauty of contrast. It's how we react to stress that brings out the best or worst in us. It's normal to feel shit at times and it's normal to sometimes be irrational but when we have a chance to be happy, embrace it with both hands. My motto for work is "Unite. Inspire. Empower." but my motto for Life is "Live. Love. Laugh.". Never underestimate the power of laughter. It raises our serotonin levels and creates buzzy feel good feelings, and the best thing about it is laughter is infectious. I was always a big giggler and was always playing practical jokes and laughing at school. It's what keeps us young at heart. It raises our energy flow and level of happiness. And who doesn't want to be happy? Look for the laughter in your adversities. It's the only way I've got through them! Soul searching can be tough but it doesn't have to be arduous as long as we remember to Live. Love and Laugh. Happiness is truly the key to attracting positivity into our lives. Who's up for that?

Live. Love. Laugh.

Write down five things that make you happy.

1) _____

2) _____

3) _____

4) _____

5) _____

Did you...?

E.g. 1) Accept a compliment? Yes, the postman told me he liked my new hair colour and it felt fricking awesome! Somebody noticed!

1) Smile at a stranger today?

2) Do something you've never done before?

3) Make somebody laugh?

4) Appreciate nature?

5) Tell someone you loved them?

6) Accept a compliment?

7) Put yourself first?

8) Treat yourself to a self-care luxury?

9) _____

10) _____

11)_____

The more we turn our attention to positive things that make us feel good, the more open we are to receiving more positive vibrations, circumstances and people into our lives.

- Live your life.
- Have fun.
- Learn from nature.
- Care for yourself deeply.

The more we Love and accept ourselves the more we will exude a sense of self-worth. There is nothing more attractive than a woman, or man, who knows their true value. This is not arrogance but a quiet understanding that we have the freedom of choice to reflect all that is beautiful and positive within this world or not, that we are unique and that there will never again be a person in this world quite like you, flaws, quirks and all.

We have a choice to value and honour this truth and celebrate our temporary place in this world or sink into negative thought patterns that create stories about who we are according to our past. When we cut the negative ties to the past and learn from our experiences we become lighter and freer people with the ability to inspire and shine a light in others. When we feel good about ourselves, listen to ourselves and take care of ourselves, we will begin to attract all that is positive into our lives. It's really that simple. It's a journey and we will never get it "right" all of the time, we may never feel "positive" and "happy" all of the time but by knowing who we are - what makes us happy, what we stand for and knowing our True Value, we will never be in "pursuit of happiness" but consistently on the path to Joy.

Notes:

Quiz Answers

Can You Spot a Serial Liar?

When a person is lying the evidence can usually be found in:
a) Type of words that are used
b) Non-verbal expression
c) Pitch and tone of voice

The addition of an epilogue when recounting events is a sign of:
a) A true story
b) A false story
c) Both

A person who is lying often recounts a story:
a) Starting from the end and ending with beginning
b) No sequential order
c) Using strict chronological order

A false smile uses:
a) All the muscles in the face
b) Only the muscle around the eyes
c) Only the muscles around the mouth

When recounting information liar will:
a) Use limited hand gestures
b) Over exaggerate hand gestures
c) Sit on their hands

When lying a liar will often touch:
a) Chest, arms, hands
b) Face, mouth, throat
c) Legs, feet and ankles

A common gesture for a liar is:

    a) Interlocking hands behind their head

    b) Scratching their nose or ear

    c) Nodding incessantly

When liar's story will:

    a) Contain lots of emotion

    b) Lack emotion

    c) Contain lots of detail

Liars commonly leave out words like:

    a) Pronouns- I, me, my

    b) Adjectives-describing words like beautiful, amazing, exhilarating

    c) Adverbs- slowly, happily, excitedly

A real smile uses:

    a) Lower half of face

    b) The muscles around the mouth area

    c) All the muscles in the face

www.ingramcontent.com/pod-product-compliance
Lightning Source LLC
Chambersburg PA
CBHW080953050426
42334CB00057B/2615